Herb Gardening For Beginners

How To Effectively Start Gardening and Harvesting Herbs Easily

Disclaimer
- Although the author and publisher have made every effort to ensure that the information in this book was correct at press time, the author and publisher do not assume and hereby disclaim any liability to any party for any loss, damage, or disruption caused by errors or omissions, whether such errors or omissions result from negligence, accident, or any other cause.
- This book is not intended as a substitute for the medical advice of physicians. The reader should regularly consult a physician in matters relating to his/her health and particularly with respect to any symptoms that may require diagnosis or medical attention.

Copyright 2014 by Barbara Glidewell - All rights reserved.

This document is geared towards providing exact and reliable information in regards to the topic and issue covered. The publication is sold with the idea that the publisher is not required to render accounting, officially permitted, or otherwise, qualified services. If advice is necessary, legal or professional, a practiced individual in the profession should be ordered.

- From a Declaration of Principles which was accepted and approved equally by a Committee of the American Bar Association and a Committee of Publishers and Associations.

In no way is it legal to reproduce, duplicate, or transmit any part of this document in either electronic means or in printed format. Recording of this publication is strictly prohibited and any storage of this document is not allowed unless with written permission from the publisher. All rights reserved.

The information provided herein is stated to be truthful and consistent, in that any liability, in terms of inattention or otherwise, by any usage or abuse of any policies, processes, or directions contained within is the solitary and utter responsibility of the recipient reader. Under no circumstances will any legal responsibility or blame be held against the publisher for any reparation, damages, or monetary loss due to the information herein, either directly or indirectly.

Respective authors own all copyrights not held by the publisher.

The information herein is offered for informational purposes solely, and is universal as so. The presentation of the information is without contract or any type of guarantee assurance.

The trademarks that are used are without any consent, and the publication of the trademark is without permission or backing by the trademark owner. All trademarks and brands within this book are for clarifying purposes only and are the owned by the owners themselves, not affiliated with this document.

Your FREE Gift

Click Here

As a way of saying thank you,
Get your free natural therapeutic remedies report by clicking below.

What you'll receive

Enjoy the rest of the book!

Click here to get your Natural Therapeutic Remedies Report

Table Of Contents

Your FREE Gift 4

Table Of Contents 5

Introduction 6

Chapter 1. Herbs – A brief history 7

Chapter 2. Gardening basics 8

Chapter 3. The Life of an Herb 10

Chapter 4. Planting Herbs 11

Chapter 5. Harvesting 13

Chapter 6. Proper Stock and Storage 14

Conclusion 16

Introduction

Gardening, with any kind of plant life, should be viewed as a relaxing and fulfilling activity. It not only brings you closer to Earth, but also allows you to have a somewhat intimate relationship with it. There's a different kind of satisfaction there, being that close to nature, understanding the workings of this life form and forging a symbiotic relationship with the elements.

For there is such a joy to gardening and, as you delve into the foundations of this ancient ritual of planting, caring, and, finally, harvesting, you will find happiness in the fruits of this bountiful Earth.

We will explore the different techniques in gardening that you can learn as a beginner. We will touch on the different perils of this activity and how to best overcome if not avoid them. We are going to learn the intricacies of herbs and what makes them tick—how they survive and how they acquire their most pungent and aromatic flavors that tickle our palates.

In this book, we will introduce you to the world of Herb Gardening and show you how delightful it is to grow your own herb garden. If you have no knowledge of gardening as a whole, do not worry, we will provide basic and easy to follow instructions on how you can begin this beautiful journey and, more importantly, how to see it through. Soon, you will revel in the delights of a kitchen full of fresh, aromatic, and flavorful herbs that nothing, but the herbs from your own garden, will ever satisfy your palate.

Then again, why stop there? If you grow enough, perhaps you can start distribution—why not? Herbs are quite expensive, especially if grown naturally and organically. If you can earn while ensuring your own home's supply then that makes the deal even sweeter, doesn't it?

So, make yourself a cup of tea (or coffee), sit in your most comfortable chair, and let us take you on a wonderful trip into herb gardening.

Chapter 1. Herbs – A brief history

In order to appreciate herb gardening a bit more, we should look at how it all began. Let us talk about a brief background on herbs and their use in our society.

When did we start using them?

Well, no one knows for sure, but I'm guessing they've been around for quite some time—about a few thousand years, perhaps. It is quite possible that humans discovered plants and their usage ahead of hunting for meat simply because it was easier to gather vegetation around them than to kill animals. It is not only less dangerous, but plants were in abundance. Cultivating the earth to yield more produce was possibly among the first skills mankind had to learn and master.

So, herb gardening must have been very popular if not essential to the ancient world. It was where they got most of their food from and what they used mainly in curing diseases. This trait has been handed down history to our modern day, which is why it is making such a huge comeback now. People are again seeing the sense in growing their own plants and there's no better way to start your gardening adventure than by planting herbs! You not only get the satisfaction of harvesting them for your food, but you also have the beginnings of your own all natural pharmacy!

Chapter 2. Gardening basics

Alright! Let's start with a basic knowledge of this thing called *gardening*. What you need to know is that it all starts and ends with the elements: earth, sun, water, and air. All are essential to grow any kind of plant life in any sort of garden.

Something notable about herbs is the fact that most if not all—have their origins from countries that enjoy a lot of sun. Many herbs have their historical beginnings from the Mediterranean regions as well as Asia. There is such a thing as too much sun and too little, so it will help dramatically if you will learn how much sun is too much for that herb before starting your garden.

If you have a lot of open space with dirt, find a spot where there's enough sunlight to bathe you in warm, but not scorching, heat. Most plants will wilt when exposed to the burning heat of an afternoon sun, so find a spot where a plant can drink in morning sunlight and be shaded in the afternoons.

Watering is also an essential part of gardening and, quite notably, one that has been misapplied by many. People think that plants, like humans, would require a constant intake of fluids. The answer is yes and no. Yes, they do need water, and they do need it constantly—but on a daily basis, and this depends on the humidity and climate in your place. So, once a day watering is already quite sufficient for a plant to grow. They do not need to be drenched in water. As long as the soil remains damp the whole day to allow them to drink from the soil, most plants will not only survive but thrive. So, water when you should, and try not to overdo this because too much water will drown plants, too.

Air is also needed. Plants give off oxygen (which is what we need) and in turn, we give off carbon dioxide (which is what they need). With that in mind, there should be plenty of space for plants to "breathe" in the air they need. Do not overcrowd a container with so many seedlings or plants. They will suffocate. There should be enough space for plants to grow and for air to circulate to allow the plant to breathe freely. It is also good to loosen the soil in the container to allow air to circulate more.

To ensure you have healthy soil, you can purchase bags of potting soil from your nearest gardening shop or you can do it yourself. All you need is compost (you can make some yourself, or buy ready-made. If you're going to make some yourself try using organic material like leaves, peels of fruits and vegetables, etc. These make better compost material and are healthier for plants), and then mix it with the soil in your own garden. The compost will balance out the pH levels of the soil, turning it into rich soil ready for planting.

Now that you have the elements ready, you also need to have tools. The basic gardening tools are shovels (small spades will also help for smaller plots and containers), shears, gloves, spray bottles, watering cans, soil fork, garden buckets, and a hand weeder.

Alright, gardener! Now that you are equipped, let us learn a bit more about herbs.

Chapter 3. The Life of an Herb

Herbs have different life cycles or seasons. There are herbs that only last for one season while there are others that last as long as forever. So, let's talk about the seasons of herbs.

Once it has given off enough seeds to propagate the species, it will finally die. Biennial herbs cannot survive adverse weather conditions, which means you will have to choose the exact months of planting in order to harvest as much from these herbs as you can before the end of their life cycle.

An annual herb is one that begins and finishes its life cycle or season in a year. You don't have to feel bad about them, that is how they were created. There are two kinds of annual plant life: summers and winters. Summers germinate in spring and come to full maturity by fall within that same year. Winters germinate during fall and mature in either spring or early summer the following year.

Annual herbs will give you a good harvest within its life cycle and then start seed or flower production in preparation of its nearing end.

Chapter 4. Planting Herbs

We have now come to the most exciting part—planting! Let's start with location and containers.

For large spaces, raised beds are preferable because this allows the water to drain better. It also makes it easier to weed them since you don't need to stoop a lot. You can also use large clay pots (some even go wild with their choices of pottery) or you can use old unused items like a busted kettle, an old leather shoe or boots, baskets, tin cans, wooden boxes, and plastic containers. For indoor gardening, choose smaller containers that have good drainage.

Now, depending on the climate, you have to check your pots to ensure that they have not dried up. Once you see course earth that means the seeds are begging for water. Now, do not be overzealous and drench them. Again, just spray evenly across, making sure the soil is damp enough and not soaked. It is also crucial during this stage that you do not move the soil about. Allow the seeds to germinate and take root.

A big problem for gardeners the world over are pests. These are insects that infest your garden and cause your herbs to get sick. It is a job to remove them and another to treat infected plants.

How do you deal with pests in your herb garden? As much as possible, we encourage you to use organic solutions and not chemical pesticides since herbs—well, the main reason for planting them—are for human consumption. Any chemical pesticide will penetrate the plant and make unfit for eating, storing, or brewing. Then again, you may think that if the infestation is severe then the only way to resolve this is by using harmful chemicals.

If the problem is so bad that you have no other course available but to use chemical pesticides, I would suggest to just remove all the plants and start new. It is better to be safe than sorry. Pesticides will kill the creepy crawlies infesting your garden, but they will also render your herbs inedible. Just remove the, start fresh, and this time watch over the garden better.

One method is by using an organic spray that will repel pests and still encourage healthy growth to help the herbs fight diseases on their own. There are many in the market nowadays, one very popular choice is seaweed spray. It has lots of vitamins, minerals, and nutrients essential for herbs to grow healthier and sturdier, helping them fight off diseases. Seaweed spray is also known to keep slugs away.

Another technique is to move your plants about. Displacing them or rotating them in your garden will prevent another infestation. Remember that pests prefer specific plants, and detest others. So, moving them into areas where there are natural repellents will prevent the infestation from spreading.

If you also notice weak plants in your pots or beds, remove them. They may be infecting other healthier members of the group, and they attract pests. Pull them out by the roots and discard them as far away from your garden as possible.

Now, we don't use strong pesticides for the herbs themselves, but you have to disinfect the tools you use. Clean your tools before and after you use them in your garden. If one part of your garden is heavily infected or infested, clean your tools before using it on another part of your garden that is free of pests. This way you prevent the spread of diseases and pests among the plants.

When it comes to fertilizers, it is best to stick with organic ones. In this aspect, again, you use use your own (like compost) or purchase some from your local garden specialty shop. Use it sparingly, though. If you are to purchase fertilizers, read as much about them before you buy. Try to find out how much to use and how often.

When the herbs start showing bushy, rich green foliage, well, then it's time to harvest!

Chapter 5. Harvesting

A very important reminder when it comes to harvesting your herbs is to never harvest more than a third of the leaves at a time. This will allow the plant to recover because after all you were invasive, removing parts of it. So, be kind; take only what you need and leave some for the plant to recover from the shock of losing its leaves.

Now, for annual herbs, you can pick the leaves as you need, but you can also harvest them as a whole. Anyway they will be dying soon, so you can do an annual harvest of the entire plant.

When the herbs start flowering (in preparation for propagation), harvest the flowers as well, but this time go as far as bottom level—as in as close as you can get to the soil.

When to harvest is also a good thing to know. Can you harvest at any time? Well, herbs are appreciated more because of their essential oils, seeds, or flowers. To make sure you are harvesting the herbs at their best, you have to pick the leaves early in the morning, just after the delicious morning dew has dried up. The most flavorful leaves are the ones that were picked right after the plant flowers (before the buds open), so if you have biennial or annual herbs, wait for them to bloom to harvest the leaves you will use for long storage or for drying.

So to find out how to properly harvest your herbs (from leaves to seeds), read up on them and get to an almost intimate level with their personalities.

Chapter 6. Proper Stock and Storage

I can think of three ways to properly stock and store herbs: fresh, dry, frozen.

To store fresh herbs, divide them into two categories. Soft herbs (this includes cilantro or coriander, basil, parsley, and tarragon) and hard herbs (these are thyme, oregano, marjoram, and rosemary). Store herbs that belong in the same category together.

For hard herbs, do not wash them if you are planning to store them because this will add moisture to the leaves that you don't need. Wash them when you are ready to use them. If you plan to store them, what you do is collect them in a bunch and, using a damp (not wet) paper towel, wrap your herbs and cover with plastic wrap or put inside a zippy bag. Keep this in the crisper section of your fridge.

For soft herbs, you can keep them fresh by putting them in a vase with water (like you would flowers). Cut of the base stems before you put the in the vase and change the water daily. Make sure that the temperature in the room where they are kept does not exceed room temperature or these will wilt. If you put them in the refrigerator, cover the bouquet of herbs loosely with plastic before putting the entire vase inside the fridge.

When drying herbs for storage, you have to know the kinds of herbs that you can dry. Woody herbs like rosemary, thyme, and marjoram—herbs that belong to the hard category—are the best candidates for dry storage. They don't have a lot of moisture compared to the other herbs. I will not encourage you to dry herbs that belong in the soft category for this type of storage simply because they do have a lot of moisture and not only will it take a long time for them to dry up, but they can also get moldy within the process.

It is best to air dry herbs and you can do this by hanging them upside down by the stems in your kitchen or in a cool, well-ventilated, but dry place away from direct sunlight. Drying can take up to two weeks and you will know they are ready when you pinch the leaves and they are brittle and crisp in your fingers. To store herbs frozen, some people also use ice cube trays. If you don't like that you can also use the cookie sheet style. What you need to remember, though, is that herbs should be frozen individually before putting them in containers. This is why we use a cookie sheet for this initial process. Make sure the herbs are clean and dry before freezing. When you put the herbs on the cookie sheet, separate them so that they do not freeze in clumps. Cover the cookie sheet and place it in the freezer. Once they are good and solid, then you can store them in containers, preferably airtight, and return them into the freezer. Frozen herb flavors are not as concentrated as dried herbs. Actually, they have the same level of flavor as fresh herbs.

Conclusion

Hopefully, by now, you have been properly encouraged to start your herb garden. It is not really difficult and you are under no obligation to plant all the herbs under the sun. That's the beauty with starting your own garden: you get to choose the plants you actually like! So pick a favorite—maybe an herb that you love to eat or cook with? Or something that is easier to manage? Then again, you may be brave enough for something is challenging. Whatever your choice it is yours to make. What we've laid out for you here is just a simple and basic guide to herb gardening. We wanted to give you the tools and basic information you need to start you off. Why don't we have a recap of the things we've discussed so far?

Well, you have been given a brief trip down history first to give you a bigger perspective and help you develop an appreciation for herbs in general. Then, we gave you the basic of what you need to start a garden. All the tools and essential ingredients needed were properly laid out for you so you can start it right.

With all this information the only remaining step is application. Try it out, start small, and build your garden as you go along. Before you know it, you will have an unquestionable Eden-like garden filled with aromatic herbs ready for you to harvest, store, and enjoy!

A PREVIEW OF :

Medicinal Plants

A Beginner's Guide to Learning the Benefits of Organic Herbs and Plants

Disclaimer
- Although the author and publisher have made every effort to ensure that the information in this book was correct at press time, the author and publisher do not assume and hereby disclaim any liability to any party for any loss, damage, or disruption caused by errors or omissions, whether such errors or omissions result from negligence, accident, or any other cause.
- This book is not intended as a substitute for the medical advice of physicians. The reader should regularly consult a physician in matters relating to his/her health and particularly with respect to any symptoms that may require diagnosis or medical attention.

Copyright 2014 by Barbara Glidewell - All rights reserved.

This document is geared towards providing exact and reliable information in regards to the topic and issue covered. The publication is sold with the idea that the publisher is not required to render accounting, officially permitted, or otherwise, qualified services. If advice is necessary, legal or professional, a practiced individual in the profession should be ordered.

- From a Declaration of Principles which was accepted and approved equally by a Committee of the American Bar Association and a Committee of Publishers and Associations.

In no way is it legal to reproduce, duplicate, or transmit any part of this document in either electronic means or in printed format. Recording of this publication is strictly prohibited and any storage of this document is not allowed unless with written permission from the publisher. All rights reserved.

The information provided herein is stated to be truthful and consistent, in that any liability, in terms of inattention or otherwise, by any usage or abuse of any policies, processes, or directions contained within is the solitary and utter responsibility of the recipient reader. Under no circumstances will any legal responsibility or blame be held against the publisher for any reparation, damages, or monetary loss due to the information herein, either directly or indirectly.

Respective authors own all copyrights not held by the publisher.

The information herein is offered for informational purposes solely, and is universal as so. The presentation of the information is without contract or any type of guarantee assurance.

The trademarks that are used are without any consent, and the publication of the trademark is without permission or backing by the trademark owner. All trademarks and brands within this book are for clarifying purposes only and are the owned by the owners themselves, not affiliated with this document.

ANY ISSUES WITH THIS BOOK, COPYRIGHT, OR ANY OTHER ISSUES, PLEASE EMAIL RANDYCFO@TRIGGERHEALTHYHABITS.COM

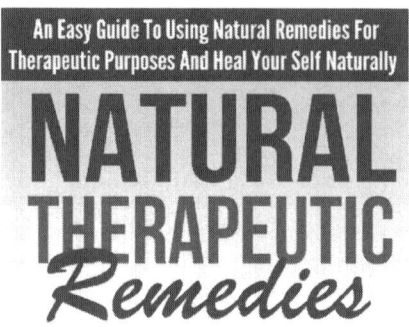

Your FREE Gift
Click Here
As a way of saying thank you,
Get your free natural therapeutic remedies report by clicking below.
What you'll receive
Enjoy the rest of the book!

Click here to get your Natural Therapeutic Remedies Report

Table Of Contents

Table Of Contents

Introduction

Chapter 1: A Guide to Medicinal Plants

Chapter 2: Herbs for Common Ailments

Chapter 3: Herbs for Respiratory Health

Chapter 4: Herbs to Aid Digestion

Chapter 5: Healing Herbs for Faster Recovery

Chapter 6: Herbs for Skin Problems

Conclusion

Thank you and good luck!

Introduction

Common herbs and spices can help ward off chronic illnesses like cold, flu, digestive problems and even high blood pressure. Most people use herbs and plants as seasoning to their dishes. While this has its own advantage, herbs also have very potent medicinal value.

Herbal medicine is a lot cheaper than conventional medicine. It also has fewer side effects compared to drugs sold in the market. Herbs are also highly versatile. You can use their oil extracts in aromatherapy or apply these topically onto skin. It can also be made into various products like anti-acne and anti-wrinkle creams.

Harnessing the power of herbs is very empowering. It gives you the ability to prevent or control unwanted symptoms. Also, whipping up your own medicinal concoction can be educational and fun.

Chapter 1: A Guide to Medicinal Plants

Herbal remedies are becoming very popular even when modern science seems to be thriving. Most people rely on herbal medicine and organic herbs as their first remedy for common illness. There are also people who use extremely potent plants as a last resort when their prescribed medicine is not doing enough.

Herbal medicine is the practice of using plants, seeds, berries, leaves, roots and barks for medicinal purposes. With the increasing costs of drugs being sold in the market, herbal medicine is becoming more popular. Also, there are a lot of studies that show that herbs can be very effective in treating certain conditions and diseases.

.

Benefits of Herbal Medicine

Using herbal supplements has many advantages. Here are some of the benefits of using herbs and plants as medicine.

All natural ingredients

Since these herbs are all natural, they pose less risk to the body. It is different from conventional medicine that is mixed with synthetic chemicals to increase its potency. It is also a good idea to check with your government health regulations to see if the herb is safely approved.

Minimal side effects

Most herbal medicines have few side effects since they are free from chemicals. Herbal medicine is usually less potent than chemical drugs so you can safely use it every day. You are also less likely to develop allergic reaction to herbal medicine. Make sure that your herbal medicine is 100% natural to be safe.

Cheaper by comparison

People turn to herbal medicine because it is more affordable by comparison to conventional medicine. The main reason why it is cheap because it uses natural ingredients and not synthetic ingredients which can costs more. Herbal medicine is also readily available. You can also plant your own herbs at your backyard and use it whenever you need it.

Chapter 2: Herbs for Common Ailments

After learning the benefits of herbal medicine, you might be too eager to try it out for yourself. You might be surprised that you already have enough herbs in your pantry to cure common ailments. Here are some of the herbal remedies that you can try before taking any medication.

<u>Best Herbs for Cough, Flu and Cold</u>

Black pepper

Black pepper is ideal for relieving wet cough. Black pepper is a natural cough remedy that is rooted both in New England medicine and Chinese medicine. The black pepper can stimulate circulation and mucus flow. Adding honey does not only sweeten the herbal teas but also add antibiotic benefits as well.

Cayenne pepper

Cayenne pepper is a great anti-microbial and stimulant. It has also been used as a diaphoretic and analgesic. Cayenne pepper can prevent flu and shorten its duration. It heats the body and dispels coldness.

Made in the USA
Middletown, DE
28 November 2015